AF433273

ngā whakamatuatanga/interludes

Vaughan Rapatahana

2019

Copyright© 2019 Vaughan Rapatahana
ISBN: 978-93-89074-41-3

First Edition: 2019
Rs. 200/-

Cyberwit.net
HIG 45 Kaushambi Kunj, Kalindipuram
Allahabad - 211011 (U.P.) India
http://www.cyberwit.net
Tel: +(91) 9415091004 +(91) (532) 2552257
E-mail: info@cyberwit.net

No part of this book may be reproduced or transmitted in any form or by any means, electronic, mechanical, photocopying, or otherwise, without the express written consent of Vaughan Rapatahana.

Printed at Repro India Limited.

Acknowledgements

Several of the poems in this collection have been previously published, or will be during 2019, in the following publications:

Catalyst; Mayhem; New Zealand Poetry Shelf; Takahē; Meniscus; Poetry New Zealand; Valley Micropress; Brief; Fairfax Media; L'Homme Blanc Est Venu; Fresh Ink, 2019; To End All Wars.

i) ngā wāhi/places

Waitangi, 2017

[*he waka eke noa*]

as sunrise sulks

        behind sentry clouds

refusing to grant us grace,

we traipse telluric

that scurfy scrub,

enduring h e r e & t h e r e,

like scabrous cur

too stubborn to die.

the karanga guitar solo

sustained ethereal,

is a cascade escalier

we strive to scale

in our unkempt scansion.

inside -

amid a versicolour cohort –

we koha

all cowed & bowed

in deference,

to *scrawled* sigils

& the faded tohu

inveigled   s o   m a n y   d e c a d e s   ago,

while karakia

bestow almighty

hongi to this day.

[*he waka eke noa* – Māori – we are all in this together

karanga – call

koha – gift

tohu – signature mark

karakia – prayer

hongi – press noses in greeting]

gone troppo

it isn't anything specifically pacific,

to anything much at all.

a mere gust of strategic sand

underwriting an implausible reef - or two

& a shoreline receding faster than

an old man's hair.

some palm trees palmed off

by a f l e e t i n g trader

and gulls so nondescript

they mergeintothe*shimmer*

waves just laugh

as they frappe the beach,

while the crabs seem indifferent

to such frottage.

lagoon eyelet closed

to oceanic awakening;

another   lost   islet

desu lto ril y
a   d   r   i   f   t

  seas   that   have

far   **bigger**   fish

to fry.

te araroa foreshore, mid-winter

& so it starts again,

this seedy psychodrama;

the grim simplistic sky

lamenting itself silly

across another apathetic day.

the trees forget their sway;

so nearly penitent

in their manner,

they vaunt arms-span oblation

into broken crucifix.

the weak wind whistles

its discordant syllables

to a sea bereft of ideas,

thrashing itself senseless

onto the stupid shore.

callous rain will soon trudge on in,

its cumbrous footwear

a further scourge

to flay the futile shoulders

of encroaching night.

& as for me -

                    I am but an a f t e r t h o u g h t.

a drifter gathering driftwood,

the fictionalized version

of myself,

            s h i p w r e c k e d

        amongst the sea wrack,

as dusk drowns

    my way.

waiting for the train blues (hong kong 2014)

adhered again,

to this unrelenting plinth;

the clichéd 'cast in stone',

every fractured semester

of a lapidarian life.

if birds

could – somehow –

scrounge their ways into

this cavernous crypt

they call a terminus,

their shit would

surely conjoinmyown;

indeterminate.

    got the waiting for the train blues

    taking me away again,

    got these waiting for the train blues

    maaan,

       such a goddam pain.

last bus from apia, october 2018

'talofa lava' she said,

with a grin

that trashed all of the others.

she shunted aside the kit

where the clothes

ate into the taro,

while with her feet

she banished the carton of drinks

deep under the seat in front,

till only a memory remained.

the music was marley

burrowing my eardrums

like drills in delirium,

and I smiled 'talofa',

as I perched my sunburn

beside her ample lavalava

on the staunch wooden pew.

the bus chugged on,

first d r a w i n g,

then dropping more passengers

the further we divorced the capital

'malo' & 'malo' & 'malo'

on infinite replay

as the sunshine stoked higher

& bob became bop.

'fa'afetai,' she beamed

as I contorted myself

to liberate her

and her truckload of trinkets,

to haul herself habile through

those still standing

& to drop four tala

into the driver's o u t s t r e t c h

             e

           d

             p a l m.

'fa'afetai,' I distributed

when it was my turn

to funambulate through to the front,

tala in grasp;

& to jest with

the *spring-heeled*

who helped me debark -

near the resort hotel

       with

its **exorbitant** extravagance

they'd never heed.

fa'afetai a'u uo,

fa'afetai indeed.

[talofa lava – hello to you

malo - hi

fa'afetai – thank you

a'u uo – my friends

- all Samoan]

best route to batangas

['traffic here writes itself across the page of a found poem' –
rapatahana, 2017]

> *drivin' down your freeways*
>
> *midnight alleys roam* [The Doors]

f r e e d from edsa mayhem:

the s p r e a d s of

    carton beds,

& the spinning heads

panhandling

that useless mishmash

you'll never need,

escaped the erratic

jeepster eddy,

& that louring

bus fume soup,

             o u t   o n t o   the freeway,

        our d-day;

where lives are on the line.

never felt a rhythm so bizarre

than riding in this car.

O.K., claim a lane,

fastest pedal wins,

           - gotta have that

magic swerve

           - gonna be the one

without nerve

while the *zapping* synapses

   divagate

t h r o u g h their brains

     never felt a rhythm so bizarre

     than riding in this car.

walang problema overtaking,

speed just steers you through,

ignore the signs right up ahead,

they are not meant for you.

     never felt a rhythm so bizarre

     than riding in this car.

mabilis kaibigan

batangas awaits

   &

there's 50 red horse

l i n e d   up in laiya;

    so

there's no time to be late.

[*walang problema* – no problem; *mabilis* – fast; *kaibigan* -
friend – all Tagalog]

[edsa is the congested central part of Manila city; jeepney is a
distinctive Philippine people-mover; red horse is a particularly
strong Philippine beer]

requiem for a winter's day

the day had died

during its rambunctious sleep

the night before.

no sun could be sought

t h r o u g h the legions

of lank onyx cloud

resolved belligerently to

keep spectators   well   *a   d r i f t*

the scene.

whetumatarau sneered down silent

like some retired school

principal

bereft of his desk

& with nothing else to do.

it rained a squadron of

the usual dark sharp schisms,

as cousin cold sniggered

& sneaked its wily way

through any vestige of warmth.

no one attended this *tangi*

of the waves' incessant winter;

nobody wept tears for this chill.

all were too busy coaxing flame

from bedraggled wood clumps,

more sullen, sodden

    & forlorn

than

    even

       them.

[*Whetumatarau* is a highly significant mountain over-reaching
the town of Te Araroa–Kawakawamai-Tawhiti, East Coast of
Aotearoa New Zealand

tangi - Māori - funeral]

mō ōtautahi 2019

[for Christchurch 2019]

me kāore tētahi ki te mate i roto i te ara taua

kāore tētahi

                  no one needs to die in such a way

                  no one.

I saw two swans regal glide

down the still lake

this afternoon.

they travel miraculous

one   well ahead
the other

b o t h   s e r e n e.

our dog a source of his own amusement

off on another parabola.

everyone should -

at least once -

inhale such harmony,

peace epitomized as epiphany.

me kāore tētahi kia whakamatea i roto i te ara taua

me kāore tētahi ki te whakamatea

kāore tētahi

          no one needs to kill in such a way

          no one needs to kill

          no one.

Aotearoa New Zealand

Ko Aotearoa te ingoa o tēnei whenua ātaahua.

land of the long white cloud for many

nestling in a sea of verdant green,

surrounded by a brilliant blue ocean

& where the All Blacks reign.

Yet of course New Zealand

is also the name of these islands

some say that maybe -

with our increasingly multi-cultural crew

Pākehā, Māori, Asian, Pasifika –

it is time for a new name,

stressing our interconnections?

after all, we are rowing together

in this *waka* nowadays

heading in the right direction -

learning how we can all work together

to include as well as to respect all our

sometimes confusing cultural credos

and to *kōrero* together in spite of them

in a continuous *talanoa*.

Ni hao

Talofa lava

Tēnā koe

Geddaye
Malo e lelei

As-salam alaykom

Different, yes and yet, respecting this diversity,

this contrasting, this sometime conflicting mix,

where *te Tiriti o Waitangi* was the foundation document,

where journalism has flourished for well over 150 years

with upfront news & freedom of views

in the two key tongues, *te reo Māori rāua ko te reo Ingarihi,*

& Hindi is now the fourth most spoken language -
namaste!

together we can connect and thrive.

Āe ko Aotearoa te ingoa

throughout both North and South

we are birds singing several different *waiata*

tui, takahē, kōkako, kiwi

striving to make one mighty nest;

our own place for all -

one of a kind, a very rare *huia*,

a heaven on earth.

pristine air; clean water; prime food,

scenic vistas second to none,

what else could anyone want?

Āe, ko Aotearoa te ingoa

let's be thankful about who we are

& what we have -

the sense of fair play

the spirit of helping those in need,

sharing & supporting

including one and all.

thank you my friends

kia ora taku hoa

fa'afetai outou o a'u uo

xie xie wo peng-you

salamat po mga kaibigan

shukraan lakum 'asdiqayiy

there is so much to celebrate

in this lengthy land,

tō mātou whenua tino waimarie

& we should all be proud.

[*Kotahi ano te kōhao o te ngira*

E kuhuna ai te miro ma te miro whero me te miro pango

"There is but one eye of the needle,

Through which the white, red and black threads must pass.

[Pōtatau Te Wherowhero]

listening to lorde

listening to lorde

          inside

king ludwig's beer garden;

an aural

after-image

basting a filipino band

robotically   regurgitating

karen carpenter   karen carpenter   karen
carpenter.

              & only uncle on the organ

                talks tagalog.

the existentially sullied

māori

scans baffled

the rowdy crowd

cheerfully chomping

sauerkraut & sausages

far too plump for

their plates.

here in hung shui kui,   waaaaaay out
north-west,

                              where the wind cries mary

                                beyond the mortar walls

                                  bearing coats of arms,

karen

        segues

                freddie aguilar,

        soughing

like they're

        drowning

in that chunky keg

of *lowenbrau*

labeled   cannily

        in cantonese

                                        &

                              everything

                  is   goulash.

vietnam days

[I said, war, good god, now, what is it good for?
absolutely, nothing
say it again, war, what is it good for?
absolutely, nothing, listen to me – *War* - Edwin Starr, 1970]

was last in hanoi

                        in 2014;

it rained sporadic,

as we strolled

the ludic eateries

& laconic market spots

of the old quarter.

we spied few americans.

everyone was happy.

was last in ho chi minh city

                        in 2008;

it was a hot dry season,

as we were driven

cool to củ chi

& crawled the tunnels

like sudoric rodents.

we spied few americans.

everyone was happy.

was meant to be sent to c.m.t

in 1974;

it was a dismal year,

as I conscientiously objected,

to the flagitious war

& got routinely quizzed

by fat colonels

who extolled americans.

no one was happy.

was protesting the war

in 1972

it was a schismatic year,

as I opposed our troops

battling in phuoc tuy

& got abused by

my fellow countrymen

who eulogized americans.

no one was happy.

[oh no, there's got to be a better way
say it again, there's got to be a better way- *War* - Edwin Starr,
1970]

[c.m.t – compulsory military training in New Zealand,
discontinued there after 1974]

within

[*ka mate te kāinga* – Māori – the house is dead]

within,

the roof was a falsehood

as it imploded the ceiling

& the walls cried out

in mutual agony.

the sear-smearing grime

fleeing from the ransacked stove

daunted further the tepid bulbs

disconsolately bereft of shades.

> *me ora tonu te iwi i roto i tēnei wahi*

outside,

was tortuous menace

of anfractuous gorse & incorrigible weeds

greedily espousing their unruly fiefdom

over the dislocated mailbox,

& through a flatlining fence.

in genuflection to the defiant sky.

> *me ora tonu te iwi i roto i tēnei wahi*

a mangy dog

skinnier than a miser's purse

wilted where the gate

might have been,

its eyes gesticulations bereft of hope,

embodying and emboldening

this stark grimace of a place,

this forgotten neglect

too far gone to restore

& too close to ignore.

me mate te iwi i roto i tēnei wahi

[*me ora tonu te iwi i roto i tēnei wahi* – Māori - and people still live in this place

me mate te iwi i roto i tēnei wahi – and people die in this place]

[Note: The original *whakatukī* or proverb is *ka mate te kāinga tahi, ka ora te kāinga rua* (When one house dies, a second lives). Sadly, and badly, this was not the case here. This poem concerns my anguish at witnessing people live in such an environment in Aotearoa New Zealand in the 21st century, and nothing being done about it.]

Rangiaowhia, 1864

[I pāhuatia ō mātou tūpuna i Rangiaowhia - our ancestors
were killed unguarded and defenseless at Rangiaowhia –
Tom Roa, 2014].

ko wai e mōhio mo ngā whakapiko o Rangiaowhia?

kāore te maha ki tēnei whenua ināianei.

ko wai e mahara ngā tamariki mura

kāore te maha o tēnei rohe.

ko wai e whakapono te kupu o ngā mōrehu?

ko he tokoiti anake o ngā iwi kei mōwaho tēnā tāone.

Auē.

   Auē.

      Auē.

ki ngā hāhi hoki,

ki ngā hāhi hoki,

te wāhi puaroa; te wāhi whakaruruhau -

tēnei rīri whakamataku o ngā pākehā.

tēnei tārukenga nā ngā tāngata mā.

kia mōhio ki tātou katoa.

[Note: At dawn on February 21, 1864, armed cavalry, followed
by foot troops, charged into the settlement of Rangiaowhia,
whose terrified, startled and screaming residents ran for their
lives in every direction... Rangiaowhia was a place of refuge
for women, children and the elderly. It was an open village,
lacking fortifications or defences of its own... For the
Kingitanga supporters urged to fight in a 'civilised' manner,
just like the British, the assault on Rangiaowhia was an almost
incomprehensible act of savagery. They had complied with
requests to move their families out of harm's way, only for the
troops, to deliberately target them in the most horrific manner
possible. – Vincent O'Malley, 2017].

[Translation from te reo Māori to English –

Rangiaowhia

who knows about the murders at Rangiaowhia?

not the majority in this country nowadays.

who remembers the burned children?

not the majority in this district.

who believes the word of the survivors?

only a minority of people outside that town.

alas

    alas

alas.

in the churches also

in the churches also.

the sacred place, the safe place.

this terrible deed of the pākehā

this massacre by the white men.]

ii) ngā whanaungatanga/relationships

she

she has a fierce body

it wants to eviscerate

        mine,

masticate

   &

macerate what   might   remain

those daffodils on the shelf never *wilt*

after her repast

she will gleam

& grin & glisten

and turn to other things

of more substance.

they are plastic surrogate, after all

sometimes - as she listens -

her fingernails complete an arc

& refrain from   further

p o r t i o n s -

just indicate

                    my dull bones

r e f l e x l v e l y.

while they still bloom,

disinterested.

if it had been love...

if it had been love

     you w e r e   after

I'd have gushed you 1000 barrels a day

in crude recrudescence

           [with production upped in spring]

liquid tonnes of prime grade emolument   f o r
e v e r.

[HYPERBOLIC GUSHING.]

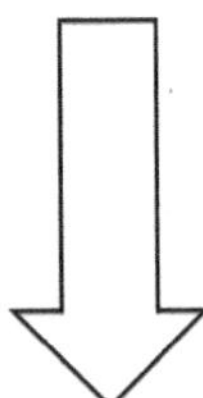

crucibles immense potboilers,

scaffolds skycrawling beyond

thor's bacchanal hammers

smashing each mighty pump

petulant/pendulant

   further through

deserted desert crust,

scarifying the hawks and few hardy rogues

who habitate such sandy climes:

with bezazz beyond compare.

I'd employ troupes of grimy troopers

regaled in sweaty bandanas,

cyclopean against such sultry effervescence

& staunch in their defence

of such grandiloquence.

there'd be a tectonic plate railroad

steering its iron way horizonless

over such tribolite vista

& the babble of this babel

would be mere droplet

in my oceanic scope.

[BUT LET'S GET DIRT REAL.]

                                                                          if only it

had been only love

                                                                       you

were after

                                                                        & not

my very grist;

                                                                        the

gutted gist of me

                                                                      purloined

                                                                       necrotic

far   b e y o n d

any oily plunder.

inhabit

I need to inhabit you,

to breathe through

your svelte frame,

glimpse through

those cryptic casements

of your mind,

stand braced

by the sure footing

you stride the world.

I want to live inside you,

be sheltered by

those sultry tresses,

enter that covert portico

few men ever reach,

be bounded

by the walls

you fabricate

to foist others away.

let me *r e c l i n e* by the fire

that is your heart,

insulated from

the *squalling* of

those squalorous hovels,

which

you never permit

        to ruin,

           your

              magnific

                haven.

dear father

I still remember

my gut grimace

every time your car

made its drunken passage home,

the murder of your engine

asserting your arrival.

sweating, I hid my face,

merged

      with those errant bedclothes;

mind racing

'please God, let it be all right.'

I felt that dread,

as you fumbled inside,

inflamed the lights,

cursed the cat.

never sleeping;

I waited instead

for that slow vicious prowl

past my door,

to claim the marital bed.

no bashings tonight, God?

no slow, dumb smiles tomorrow, God?

some nights still

I hear those cars.

they stop outside

as my head churns,

even though you're dead.

father was a white man

my father was a fight man.

the only war he ever fought

was the punch-up in the bedroom;

an audience of kids

suffocating the bedclothes in their fear

of the ruckus next door, resounding

through those thin walls.

my father was a white man.

for him, drinking

was the only form of exercise:

he became one of the best

practitioners in the block

& you could count on him

indulging in more praxis most evenings.

my father was a night man.

forever reliable;

after he had snored away the daylight

he slinked the dark

toward the drink,

just as the sun

went down

        on

      us all.

asian fathers

the last time I see

        my daughter-in-law

is at her husband's *tangi*; my own son.

I wish her well

on her impending return

        to her e s t r a n g e d korean father

waiting in incheon.

my step-daughter hugs me

as we leave her crying

        at hong kong airport,

her parents again embarking.

she never laments her

        runaway chinese father,

absconded who knows where?

my wife, born in pampanga,

lights a candle every death anniversary

        of her filipino father,

as   - beside his monochrome photograph -

            a sombre buddha

piously collects

the slow wax in upturned hands.

my own father was a white man

bereft of many, if any, saving graces.

I do not miss him one iota.

I remain thankful I can trace

                - on the matriarchal side -

my māori ancestors

            back to taiwan.

my daughter, born in aotearoa

            lives remote in bangalow

we rarely talk.

our communication lines desultory

ever since her brother's *tangi*,

despite my sporadic calls

on their birthdays.

entangled

in our convolute *samsara*

I catechize

obsessively

like some outcross ascetic:

what sort of asian father

                              am I?

[*tangi* – funeral – Māori]

[*samsara* - the endless cycle of birth, death, and rebirth – Sanskrit]

locked doors

each year is a portal

clasped firm behind us.

many remain staunchly locked.

I've lost their keys -

stalled as I am

in this caliginous c o r r i d o o r

where the impolite lightbulb

merely *flick ers* over my face

with its grubby fingers.

how did we meet?

why?

what did we dream of?

who are you now?

as these months diminish,

I attempt to grasp

some haft;

so as to

open   even   one   door,

     to

         find

             you

                 again.

ā te rā whānau o te wānanga

kia ora e hoa.

kia ora mō tāu tautoko.

kia ora mō tāu āwhina.

kia ora mō tāu mānawanawa.

kia ora mō tāu whakarongo.

kia ora mō tāu mōhiotanga.

kia ora mō tāu kōrerorero.

kia ora mō tāu tauoranga.

[on the birthday of the philosopher

thank you friend.

thank you for your support.

thank you for your help.

thank you for your patience.

thank you for your listening.

thank you for your knowledge.

thank you for your conversation.

thank you for your existence.]

pour Alain

we viewed him

        e v e r y w h e r e

who could not sight

        his u b i q u i t y?

the entrepôt, the MC, le chef de mission,

the chef's   right-hand man,

the maître de les parapluies

when rain jostled in

        uninvited.

p e r v a s i v e n e s s his forte.

later, we g l a n c e d around the bistro,

while France prevailed the cup:

not there.

'too busy back at his bookstore,' we hear.

we never did get to avow

our appreciation, our awe

of his munificence,

that eternally effervescent smile,

his sheer positive élan.

poor Alain.

il est morte.

yet, for us   - looking back -

such resplendent joie de vivre,

can never diminish.

il est toujours enchante.

[*il est morte* – he is dead

il est toujours enchante – he is charming forever – French]

the zephyr

[*he kōtuku rerenga tahi anake* - Māori – a white heron flies
once only]

the zephyr that is my lost son

still frisks me;

breezes me with questions

I can never reply.

the zephyr that is my dear son

taps me on the shoulder;

tells me to follow for a while,

to explain what I was doing

on the night in question.

the zephyr that is my dead son

wafts sometimes right through me;

arrests me in momentum,

causes   a   caesura:

t e a s e s   out   my   tears

through

    its

        balmy

            foehn.

note to a dead son

[*ko ngaro taku tama* - my son is lost

ko nui taku matapōuri - my sorrow is massive - Māori]

well, son

there is not a lot

to report.

I am of course a much older man,

but no more erudite for this survival.

the country remains bland and bifurcate,

and I scarcely see your sister

who relinquished these damp climes

some decades ago.

you have now been dead thirteen years,

none of which dims your presence.

I still miss you too much.

do you recall our trips to eden park?

to that paintball arena, where you shot the shit out of
me?

the grand prix track and your speed-crazed

s w e e p i n g circuits?

I do all of these; and more.

a taupe father's reflections,

ruing regrets,

& the austere fact

of your absence,

cloak me in opaque aura;

an early shroud,

which should not be.

this amaranthine angst

that

won't

ever

wane.

te hokinga ki te kainga

came back to catch

my life cast into a   bus te d

casket:

a black plastic trash sack

dis member ed   &   d i s c a r d e d

in   the   back-shed;

itself   *o v e r c a s t*

by stray *paewhenua* & *tawao*.

scraps of our past   s p l a y i n g   o u t

                                        onto

that   cra cke d   cement:

rusted keychains/useless gimmicks from d i s c o n t I n
u e d journals/

fuscous photographs from a former life:

a brick-a-brack filigree t r a c i n g our diremption.

under a doomed lightbulb,

my rheumy fingers tasted free-sample arthritis gel -

long since expired -

blindly caressed crippled wristwatches

& bygone birthday cards from our kids;

the cache of demode trinkets

a measure of my own neurotic agenda;

an absurd autistic panoply;
and yet,

                 m o r e than this,

an *atrophied* archive

of the   now

tectonic

         rift

       betw een

      u s.

ko taku whānau

ko he whānau pāwhati taku whānau

ki nui ngā whakawehewehe

mō nui ngā tau.

ko he urupā taku whānau

e putaputa ki ngā mate

o ngā tane

me ngā wāhine matapōrehu etahi o te wa.

taku wāhine i mua

taku tama i mate

he pāpara wara waipiro

me ngā hoa tino ngaro ināianei.

ko taku whānau

ko taku whānau

ko taku whānau

te ngare o he koroua.

heoi anō

ko te pai katoa.

ko taku mahi

kia tuhituhi te tika

me kia wewete ngā roimata

mō katoa o tātou ki te tangi.

nō te mea,

ki muri ngā roimata anake tātou kia kata.

[Translation from te reo Māori into English

my family

my family is a broken family

with many schisms

for many years.

my family is a cemetery

pitted with the deaths

of men

and sometimes the sadness of women.

my former wives

my dead son

an alcoholic father

and now very lost friends.

my family

my family

my family,

the kith and kin of an old man.

however

all is good.

it is my task

to write the truth

to release the tears

for all of us to cry.

because

only after the tears

can we laugh.]

ko kau te kete

'the kete is empty,'

were his own bereft words.

his head shook,

an oversized version

of one of these cheap bobbly toys

bought rashly from some two dollar shop

and stowed against the weary rear window

of a rusted jalopy.

his flailing eyes were an identikit of

the vertigo swirl on those murdered LPs

stowed déshabillé behind the tuneless piano;

while his tongue shot in and out/out and in

in slow-motion amphibian impersonation.

'poems, I can't do them anymore,'

he keened arrhythmic,

raising his arms

as if seeking absolution

for the missing muse,

the forsaken pages,

that *ramshackle* laptop

                                                       dusty on the table,

burnt out & barren,

                          w o r d l e s s.

as   o u t s i d e   - on the scrawny lawn -

                                         the anorexic dogs

whined

for the kai

    he could no longer provide.

[*ko kau te kete* - the kit is empty

kai – food – Māori]

the supervisor called

[*ko te reo o mātou te mauri o te mana Māori -*

our language is the heart and soul of being Māori]

the supervisor roared

                                me

i n t o her den,

as I was strolling by.

appropriateness, timeliness

castigated me for speaking in

my own language the day before -

'which no one else spoke in.'

she was erroneous   - our manuhiri
had donated their pepeha -

                        but I did not darken her

spew, as she regurgitated

the usual pale matter:

'I know it is your first tongue,

but here we must be bilingual.'

appropriateness, timeliness

I could/should have calmly constructed a canon

- te reo Māori is an official language in this land: te reo Ingarihi has never been

- in a Māori setting, whereby pepeha are shared, it is sedulous to respond in kind

- actually, why don't you make an effort to learn a couple of kupu, yourself?

I did not.

my despair, my sense of offence, merely wore me away.

whakamā 2018 and is there no end?

appropriateness, timeliness

yes, her intent was nescient,

yet the attack alacritous;

& the danger *schismatic,*

for this alabastrine administrator

further whitened our load.

[*manuhiri* – guests

pepeha – a set form of introduction

kupu – word

whakamā – shamed/embarrassed. However, this also is **to whiten** – all Māori]

the man in the room

the man came into the darkened bedroom. the man slinked nearer the pale-moon-swept windows. hiding deep beneath the covers did not dispel the man.

the man had rank skin and smelt like used condoms. the man carried the reek of cheap liquor like a birthright. incessantly praying over and over again did not disperse anything at all.

the man came further into the bedroom. the man was by now at the brink of the bedside. affirming earnest promises to god did not dispose of the man.

the man sniffed shots of snot like a feral cur. the man's odoriferous aura was a crime against life. feigning deep sleep did nothing whatsoever.

the air in the room had
THICKENED to torpid.

the time in the room became a dead algorithm of *speed*.

the heat in the room had now zoomed impossibly
huge.

the man muttered alien dictums possibly stolen from
satan. the man deep in the room was now rubbing his
hands. desperate bargaining with jesus made absolutely
no difference.

the man in the room was on top of the bed. the man in
the room had halitosis from hell. the man in the room
had echinate whiskers. the man in the room tasted like
mucus.

the man in the room came.

      the tang in the throat was

              now

                horribly

wrong.

      the man in the room...

    d e f l o w e r e d this young life

well   before

      it

      could

      bloom.

iii) te ao tūroa /nature

good old summer

summer

came back

with

a HUGE grin

s p r e a d e a g l e d

all over its face;

a panjandrum

paintbrush

of lucent hues

imbued

with emollient

flourish.

its chortling

prodigal sun

flayed us all

i

  n

    t

      o

happy   submission -

skin peeling,

smiles reeling,

balmy healing,

  &

a sort of

ubiquitous

mellow cadence

crooning through us all -

that winters'

frigid

casuistry

        had forced us

          to forget.

autumn

autumn grovels in;

like a demented mongrel,

sly,   *l e a n*

                         & mean.

denudes trees

in its slobber of gallous

                 g u s t s,

splaying leaves

into feral dog's dinner.

its serous snout

confutes &confuses

                    the sun;

sprays squalls,

squat showers

    &

intemperate gales,

which chill us,

ill-will us:

to cuss

    & curse

this equinoctial cur,

with a snarl

of oaths

of

  our

    own.

the afternoon

the afternoon

turned to me,

conspiratorial,

speaking of ill winds

&

hearty gales;

as if I was

part of his plot.

he winked cloudily

more than once,

lolled a thin index finger

near a twilight nostril

&

whispered of things

no innocent day

should ever hear.

toward dusk,

he slunk even closer

his foul autumnal breath

roiling what had

– until then –

been a tolerable few hours.

usurping the

opportunity

to *s p r e a d*   sun, to beam.

occluding

once and for all,

with his raspy overcast,

    &

me as the victim

of a tenebrous intrigue,

I never wanted to   weather.

death in winter

this day is a straitjacket;

       my arms pinioned

  behind

        my back

by his misanthropic gusts.

up ahead sneers

    only

a cloudy blindfold

of mirthless murk.

the mud is a security

    b r a c e l e t

clamping and *clumping* me,

as an hermetic rain helmet

d

  e

   s

    c

     e

      n

       d

      s

to encase my head

        &

I await defenseless

his

       vitriol

          light

        ning

          to

  strike.

today kills

yesterday was a damned fine chap;

he arrived without rancour,

rose the sun smiling

& charmed us warm throughout.

then you clambered

     in

  this morning,

uninvited.

a grey pestilential misanthrope.

slathers of bitter nimbus

warp our view,

thuds of distant thunder

rain our parade

    &

that chill inclement dank

testament to

your seedy malcontent.

on days like you

capital punishment

sneaks back

        into fashion;

slinks in to *whisper*

its imprecation:

'we can do
without

        this guy.'

this day is a dog

this day is a dog.

not one of those all-white

purebreds

                                    either.

instead the *scuzzy* clouds

shake their tufts of ugly fuzz

to obscure any sort of sun

　　&

the foul breath

panting from their fetid jaw

merely serves to

choke us all.

the tail wags

a few times,

each stroke

a flash of rancid rain,

as we s t r a g g l e r s

sprint for cover

on this collarless

mongrel of a day.

under the weather

the sky scanned me
    cursorily,
like I was a cheap can of beans;
today's $2 shop special

his mate, the sun
merely rolled his eyes
& refused to shift
from behind the cloudy gaze.

all this time, the rain drizzled
in sympathy with his comrades,
no sense of leniency
in this constant drip
                drip
                  drip.

& where was the wind

during this elemental fiasco?

he was merely l u r k i n g -

ready to gust me home,

as u-turned umbrella,

twisted around itself -

and indeed —

not worth

so much

       at

         all.

ngā rākau

he aha te tika mō ngā rākau?
tino noa tēnei:

te kāore ngā rākau

e kāore ngā manu.

te kāore ngā rākau

e kāore te ahotakakame.

te kāore ngā rākau

e kāore te mataora.

te kāore ngā rākau

ka katoa te mate tātou.

[Translation from te reo Māori to English –

        The trees

what is the truth about the trees?

quite simply this:

without the trees

there are no birds.

without the trees

there is no photosynthesis.

without the trees

there is no life.

without the trees

we will all die.]

iv) ngā tōrangapū rāua ko
ngā rapunga whakaaro/politics and
philosophy

debatable

so, another dialectic s u r g e,

an agitprop a r c

   a c r o s s

six   humid   teen

keeners.

speaker one

soars & sources

this full-on frolic

          &   by the time

a rebuttal stirs

I am well on the way,

conspiring against

any motion

any emotion

any scrimp of the

devotion

affirmative #3

distributes to his task of

di sma ntli n g

the negative polemic

mooted rawboned

through those past

gaunt minutes.

this contest is my own

existential   *oscillate*:

as émigré

sundered between

puerile skews and the

lost dross

of juvenilia,

where there is no winner

& any adjudicator

long since plotted

the loss.

robert mugabe is dead

robert mugabe is dead,

god didn't save the new king

      of england

& the impeachment

      of trump was

surprisingly simple.

now that duterte

has found the islamic faith

in his solitary squat cell

      &

putin is pinioned behind bars in

far-eastern siberia

let's have that HUGE party

we were all promised

when kim jong-un was

certified as mad as the hatter

& incarcerated on

christmas island last summer, -

alongside those sixteen

african presidents-for-life

diagnosed as incurably

power-crazy

arrayed in tidy rows

& making baskets

in preventative detention.

bashar al-assad, of course

cannot attend

after he whiffed

a little too much sarin

at mugabe's funeral,

while a sizeable number

of other obnoxious oligarchs

were simply not considered.

except lukashenko – of course -

who has found a job

as a short order cook

on devil's island,

since his own

deposing last may.

while we should not overlook

the apology from xi jinping,

still recovering from

plastic surgery after

his absconding to chile

secreting suitcases stuffed with US dollars.

so let us celebrate

a world without

despicable despots,

at least until the next one

        usurps the throne

            in a couple of

days.

intense summer

it was hot here today;

tino wera

& the world is conflagrating

quicker than we think.

yet, idiots across the waves

continue to flick aside

like a stray butt,

the demise of the only planet

we all share.

indeed, it is they who abnegate

sense and strive to

furnace all alive

ever more.

it was hot here today,

even the gulls were listless;

while tomorrow vows to

melt us mutant.

how can we all survive in a world

in denial

of its death?

[*tino wera* – Māori - very hot]

I'm having trouble with words

[*ko ngā raruraru ki ngā kupu nui ingarihi kāore ō taku roro*]

I'm having trouble with words,
you know
        the usual ones
            the english ones,
they bloviate me
in their revanchist fury.

I'm having difficulty with speaking,
you know
        the same-old stuff
            those english stresses,
they imbricate me
in their minatory strew.

I'm having issues with writing,
yunno

the extra script

these english letters

they resile me

in their philodox dudgeon.

I'm having trouble with words,

& their   fuscous   anglophile   peculation;

s p r e a d e a g l e d   o v e r   EVERY
poetry   page.

they're   *di sin te grat i ng*   my *da sein*

spoliating all aspects of design,

I'm going   kāpō myopic pohe   blind.

[*ko ngā raruraru ki ngā kupu nui ingarihi kāore ō taku roro –*
Māori -

the worries with the many english words not segueing into my
brain.]

ko te mutunga o te atua

[the end of god - Māori]

so, god ends here;

yet the question remains,

did god ever commence?

whose god is this anyway

& what do they mean by it?

some *eminence gris*?

or a desiccate wood idol

festooned in spider web,

entombed in some cave?

& who craves their god so completely?

who battles blind for their god,

to the detriment of other living beings?

who listens dumb about their god,

in obeisance to brain-dead TV preachers?

who expects their god

to somehow salve a distraught world

they have themselves sundered?

again,

god
ends here.

          &

this is not an inauspicious situation.

ko te mutunga o te atua

    āke ake ake

        āmine.

ko te tāima o te kenehi ināianei.

[it is the end of god forever and ever and ever amen. it is the
time of genesis now - Māori]

me & colin wilson

so when the people of the planet

decimated one another

and there were only the two of us

remaining...

I took off my gas mask,

unlatched the full body armour,

turned to colin

& asked,

'who is the outsider now?'

te hokowhitu a tū-mata-uenga

we too were there,

                                            some of us,

belated, begrudged

& shoved to malta first

     -     they did not want us in their 'european war';
                                                        until they lost
their troops.

we too perished there,

                                                        so many of

us,

languished

bravely, brazenly.

chunuk bair; hill 60; gallipoli

māori boys from some *iwi*

chanting *haka* hortatory,

that held the turks at bay,

more than any involute

                        fusillade of   fire

chunuk bair; hill 971; gallipoli

      -     the whitemen had then acclaimed our cohort;
                              acknowledged us as men,

yet conscripted those of us who

declined to fight their bloody battles.

chunuk bair; table top; gallipoli

we too   were   there,

mired/in/the/mud,

                    dying, expiring

for a king

                    who   could   n e v e r be

                                        ours'.

*'Listen, listen, the sky above, the earth below, and all the
people assembled here. The killing of men must stop; the
destruction of land must stop. I shall bury my patu in the earth
and it shall not rise again' – King Tāwhiao, 1881.*

[*te hokowhitu* – the first contingent of 140 Māori warrior
volunteers, sent in February,1915, representing

tū-mata-uenga – Māori god of war

iwi – tribe

haka- intimidatory war dance

patu – war club

King Tāwhiao – Māori king during and after Waikato land
wars. These words were repeated by his grand-daughter,
Princess Te Puea Herangi, when the NZ government
attempted to conscript Māori youth, in 1917.]

tahi kupu anake

ki he ao ki nui ngā kaitōrangapū porangi

ki he ao ki nui ngā tangata rawakore

ki he ao whakamahana o te ao

ko tūmanako te kupu.

ki he ao ki nui ngā pakanga

ki he ao o whakakonuka me apo

ki he ao ki te mate ā-moa o ngā kararehe

ko tūmanako te kupu.

ko tūmanako te kupu anake

ko tūmanako te kupu

ko tūmanako.

[Translation from te reo Māori to English

only one word

in a world of many mad politicians
in a world of many destitute people
in a world of global warming
hope is the word.

in a world of many wars
in a world of corruption and greed
in a world of the extinction of animals
hope is the word.

hope is the only word
hope is the word
hope.]

v) ngā toikupu/poetry

leaving it all up to you

[dale and grace, 1957]

'why don't you write a poem about…?'

it's not as easy as you seem to think.

they do not just cavort over the horizon towards me

loping askance some splendid lawrence of arabia
sunset.

they don't impel me to sit and type easy

their whiny wafts and wefts.

days, months, moods, modes *zip* by

with nothing/nada/nihil creating a cache in my mind,

itself PLUMP with other burdens.

this vitrine is empty.

poetry is constipation.

you are lucky to produce a good one

after weeks of strain; draining

those balky brain chemicals

    -     endorphin, dopamine, serotonin –
of any useful function.

why don't you write a poem…?

nō te mea

kāore taku āwangawanga ināianei e hoa.

e pīrangi ana ahau kia moemoe anake.

that's why,

I'm leaving it all up to you.

[*nō te mea*

kāore taku āwangawanga ināianei e hoa.

e pīrangi ana ahau kia moemoe anake.

because it's not my worry now friend,

I only want to sleep – Māori]

sometimes

s o m e t i m e s

writing a poem

is like

driving

      a   u

          n

    bus   d

            e

              r

      w a t e r,

not in any chaste clear current

but down some dirty back-street

        sewer drain

fucking itself silly into the sea.

the engine splutters a few times;

graunches the gears,

farts rancid diesel

      i

        n

          t

            o

   already oleaginous waves,

wallows

desperate for traction

   ac ross the *slimy* bed

    &

nearly drowns us all

in its s l o w

dy sle x ic

dysphoria

to budge a n y w h e r e at all.

breathe the poem

rescind the computer
eviscerate the ipad.

express the words.
perform the piece.

excoriate the typewriter
screw the mobile

enforce the message
emote the sounds.

massacre the book.
biff the standing still.

flail the arms

stomp the feet.

revoke the microphone

rebuke the lectern.

include the audience

disgorge the essence.

put aside the paper

revile the pen.

live   ev er y   fr i gg in g   sy lla ble.

breathe the poem.

so be it

it is not as if a poem *springs* expected from the
atmosphere

like one of those north korean warheads,

that surprisingly *spurt*

every so often over our heads,

rather like an ex-lover's complaint.

there is no predicated rate of appearance;

no well-worn waft,

whereby a seizure of verse lolls lambent on a page,

secure in the knowledge it has not only arrived,

but that all comprehend the gist.

what we receive instead is often the opposite:

no prodigal poet slamming the front gate

and skipping along the well-worn path,

spouting clusters of fine verse frankincense

and tumbles of rhythmic myrrh.

instead, a mere skittle of lines -

unaware one of another -

skedaddle around somewhat skew-whiff,

imploring their best

to grasp our gaze,

& even - if only for a marvellous moment -

to set us ramrod straight,

to nod enraptured,

'you got me this time.

you bastard' –

as we neglect our meals

coldly dying on their plate

beside us.

on the occasion of reading for p.e.n

I don't want to hear any more prattling lyrics about
verdant trees dancing beneath scudding clouds.
screw that shit.

          kinfolk are being massacred in christchurch

.

I don't want to read any more verbose verse
rambling forever on about a lost love or three.
screw that shit.

          kiribati is sinking steadily into the sea.

I don't want to see any more pale pampered poets
clutching a microphone like a baby's bottle.
screw that shit.

          kids continue to live in cars in winter

I do want us all to rage fulsome

& to rant articulate.

to highlight the brave ones,

such as wang quanzhang

struck and stuck in RSDL

for the past few years,

scarcely seen since:

& even then as a wan wafer

of his earlier self.

ko te toikupu te waha, te kaha

kia kōrero te tika mō ā tātou ao

āke ake ake

āmene.

[poetry is the voice, the force

to speak the truth about our world

forever and ever and ever

amen.]

[Note. RSDL is Residential Surveillance at a Designated Location. A recent PR China, rather sinister modification of incarceration without trial, often without evidence & certainly without informing the family of the victim.]

alien poet

I am so   far   outside

the spectrum.

                I am an alien poetic being.

cannot write

in   re gim ent ed

lines

cannot incorporate rote tropes

& structured stanza.   [cannot/will not]

e pirangi ana ahau kia tuhituhi ki taku reo tuatahi te
taima katoa hoki

englishisms trap me, snap me, rap me

because they incorporate/inculcate concepts

well b e y o n d my ken.

aaaaaaaaaaah is my sole reaction

aaaaaaaaaaah is how I feel

aaaaaaaaaaah is what I am

hindi ko gusto na ito tula

wo bu yao/wo bu dong.

existentially desiccated

ontologically fried

globally fraught

a fricassee of oblique ingredients;

I arrive from some other place, a planet not yet found

my tongue is trifurcate, bifurcate, complicate

while my brain does not function how you would have it
suppose to.

bugger & screw this bugger & screw this bugger & screw
this bugger & screw this

awopbopaloobopalopbamboom

set the controls for the heart of the sun

my journey, my escapade has scarcely begun.

[Translations -

e pirangi ana ahau kia tuhituhi ki taku reo tuatahi te taima katoa hoki – Māori -

I want to always write in my first language also

hindi ko gusto na ito tula – Tagalog – I don't want this poetry

wo bu yao/wo bu dong – Mandarin – I don't want/I don't understand]

reckon its time

reckon it is time

for a new poem.

not some l o n g w i n d e d agony aunt

expostulation concerning lost loves.

nor any political scything.

about iwi demise

through the flaccid field of ignorance.

koha the world something instead -

to harass their heads

for years to come;

some sharp barbed verse

that screws your eyes up every time you scan it,

that bites you hard in the bum

every time you search for succour.

forget the tropes, the tripe,

the silly pedantry about 'how' to write a poem

that some zombie prattle & preach.

concentrate on the pulse beat, the blood spurt,

the sheer evisceration

as some fishhook line disinters you

years before your grave.

& gush your epiphany:

'fuck, that's what a poem must do',

as you then kiss your lover full on the lips -

meaning it this time.

[*koha* – Māori – give]

vi) te raro/the underworld

suppressed images, too vile to share

    witless

and scared shitless

they sear across the pages

of my dank mind,

     black

scurrying beetles

before a deluge.

seeking shifty corners,

some refuge

    from

recognition

& well-concealed

from the spits of light

day clumps duly.

curses merely

close them denser

jampacked/awry,

in tenacious stasis,

thrusting bristles,

merely masking,

only dampening

their

clutching

poise,

of

eyes-clench poison,

talons razors

and so brazen,

readying

steadying,

     a

rampage shard of

blind-spot eddies,

their

white-hot needles

threading pincers

                              M

back home through

                              E

scalding

conscious

these *frantic stabs*

of distraught

   torture:

   boreing grabs

of sinister

   tableaux

suppressed/repressed

   de   **ing**

    press

koromiko suicide

even the cattle, mewling like old men

at the local RSA,

soon *skittled* sideways,

found something else to do,

as I raised the barrel

that little bit higher

toward a throbbing temple

just asking to be shot.

the asinine grass

beneath my skinny knees

had already pissed itself in dew

& a mid-autumn chill merely

trilled its head off,   at my expense.

above – somewhere I could not see, even if I looked –

was an absentee landlord moon

freestyling through an apathetic night;

his stars a grotesquery of gymnasts

swaying in their stele

      &

fated to *falter.*

the bullets, ah the bullets

were gibbering & jabbering away

like starving macaques,

while my tongue became a lizard

and my palms, ah my palms

were sweating seas

as their fingers

faltered on the trigger.

no final resting place

no fulcrum to finish the job,

from forehead to just behind a timid ear,

even coerced deep in chin scrolls -

the rifle could not kill myself,

near a gutless fence,

in a back paddock

showing as much concern

as a nugatory security guard

scratching his nuts

outside a shop façade.

meanwhile,

that gossipy note

left adrift on a bedroom drawer,

had led

its own breezy putsch

& now

roiled contingent

    on

the deaf ears

of the floor.

I want a good death

I want a good death.

a copacetic death -

not one of those namby-pamby

flickers of regret,

parading a pantheon of tears.

I won't rage fulsome

in dull dudgeon

against some attributed cause

for my demise,

nor slink quick like a gecko

into sudden stiff cadaver.

surround me,

with melisma of music,

friends feasting

& drinking my dip   *a w a y*   from this life -

laughing untrammelled,

as my fingers untwine

from loved ones' grip

& my eyes greet   what   is

                              next

on the list.

takoha me

a fine death

a good death.

the best death there is.

[*takoha* – Māori - give]

www.ingramcontent.com/pod-product-compliance
Lightning Source LLC
Chambersburg PA
CBHW020527160726
47992CB00005BA/2283